The Fixer's Guide to... WHEELS

Written by JOHN WOOD

Designed by AMY LI

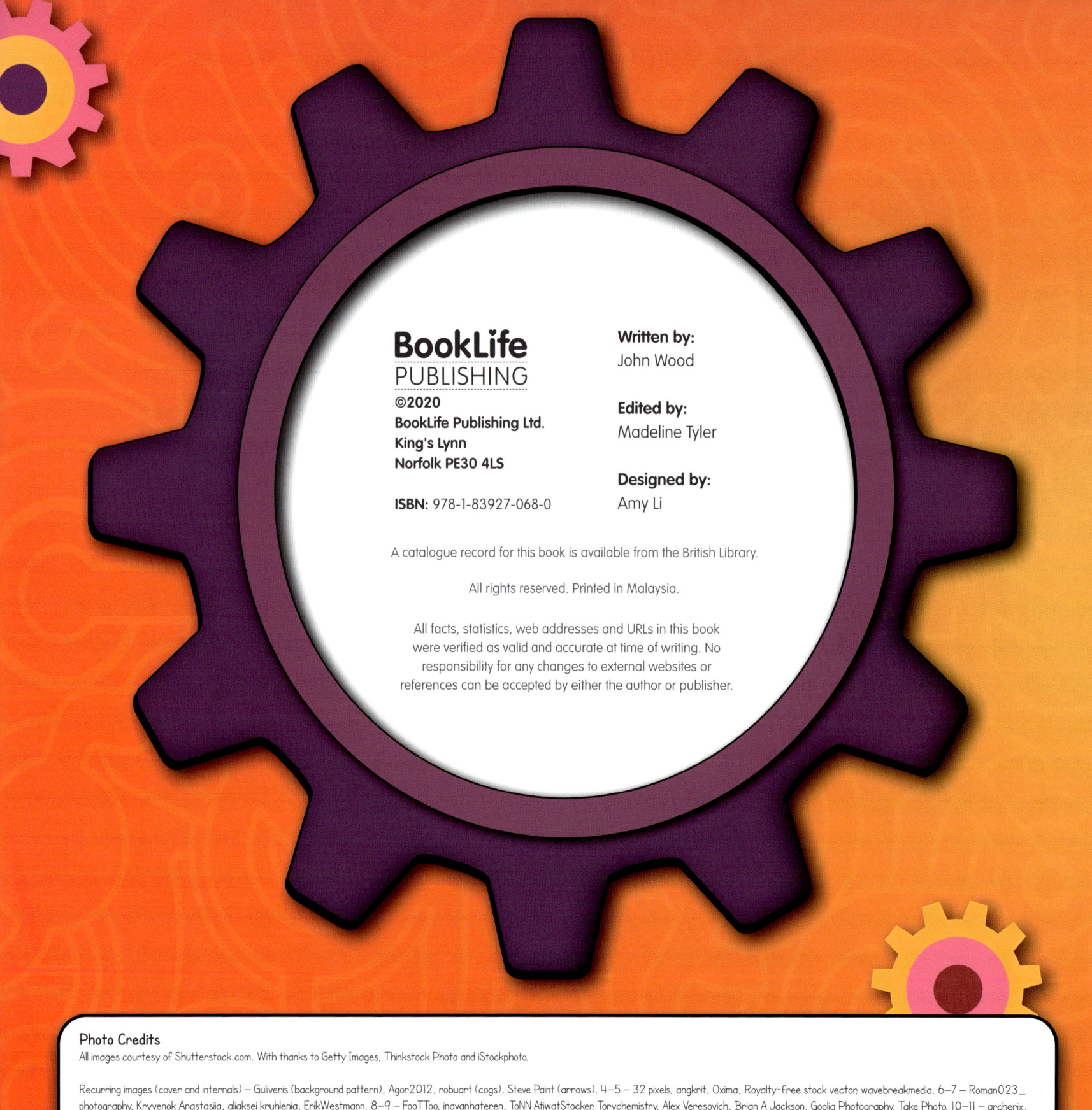

BookLife PUBLISHING

©2020
BookLife Publishing Ltd.
King's Lynn
Norfolk PE30 4LS

ISBN: 978-1-83927-068-0

Written by:
John Wood

Edited by:
Madeline Tyler

Designed by:
Amy Li

A catalogue record for this book is available from the British Library.

All rights reserved. Printed in Malaysia.

All facts, statistics, web addresses and URLs in this book were verified as valid and accurate at time of writing. No responsibility for any changes to external websites or references can be accepted by either the author or publisher.

Photo Credits

All images courtesy of Shutterstock.com. With thanks to Getty Images, Thinkstock Photo and iStockphoto.

Recurring images (cover and internals) – Guliveris (background pattern), Agor2012, robuart (cogs), Steve Paint (arrows). 4–5 – 32 pixels, angkrit, Oxima, Royalty-free stock vector, wavebreakmedia. 6–7 – Roman023_photography, Kryvenok Anastasiia, aliaksei kruhlenia, ErikWestmann. 8–9 – FooTToo, inavanhateren, ToNN AtiwatStocker, Torychemistry, Alex Veresovich, Brian A Jackson, Goolia Photography, Take Photo. 10–11 – archerix, Gorvik. 12–13 – Andrii Bezvershenko, strajinsky, Vitalliy. 14–15 – pedalist, Eganova Antonina, ABB Photo. 16–17 – hvostik, Pongchart B, supergenijalac, tcharts. 18–19 – angkrit, Oxima, Royalty-free stock vector.

CONTENTS

PAGE 4	Meet the Fixer
PAGE 6	Wheels
PAGE 10	Parts of a Wheel
PAGE 12	How a Wheel Works
PAGE 14	Friction
PAGE 16	Better Wheels
PAGE 18	Let's Build a Toy Car
PAGE 24	Glossary and Index

Words that look like this can be found in the glossary on page 24.

MEET THE FIXER

Oh no! Sorry about this mess — the Fixer can be a bit clumsy sometimes. Say sorry, Fixer.

Pfflblululupgh.

Believe it or not, the Fixer is the smartest being in the universe when it comes to machines.

A machine is an object that makes a job easier to do. The Fixer wants to teach you about one of the simplest types of machine: a wheel.

A wheelchair is a machine. And so is a car.

WHEELS

Wheels are flat and circular. They are often used to help <u>vehicles</u> move across the ground. Wheels come in lots of different sizes for lots of different jobs.

Thin, light wheels

Big, strong wheels

Hfffpflluuugh.

Axle

A wheel has a long, thin rod that goes through the middle. This rod is called an axle. The axle allows the wheel to spin round.

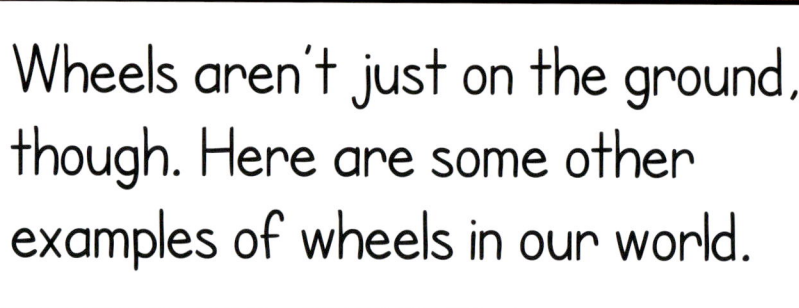

Wheels aren't just on the ground, though. Here are some other examples of wheels in our world.

Water wheel

Ferris wheel

Playground roundabout

Hamster wheel

Steering wheel

Mouse wheel

Wheels are inside lots of machines, too. They do all sorts of things.

This fan is a type of wheel and axle.

This doorknob is a wheel and axle too.

PARTS OF A WHEEL

Pffflubleulblu.

The Fixer says he wants to show you the parts of a wheel.

Wheel

Some wheels have spokes, like these.

Many wheels used for vehicles have rubber tyres, like this one.

Axle

10

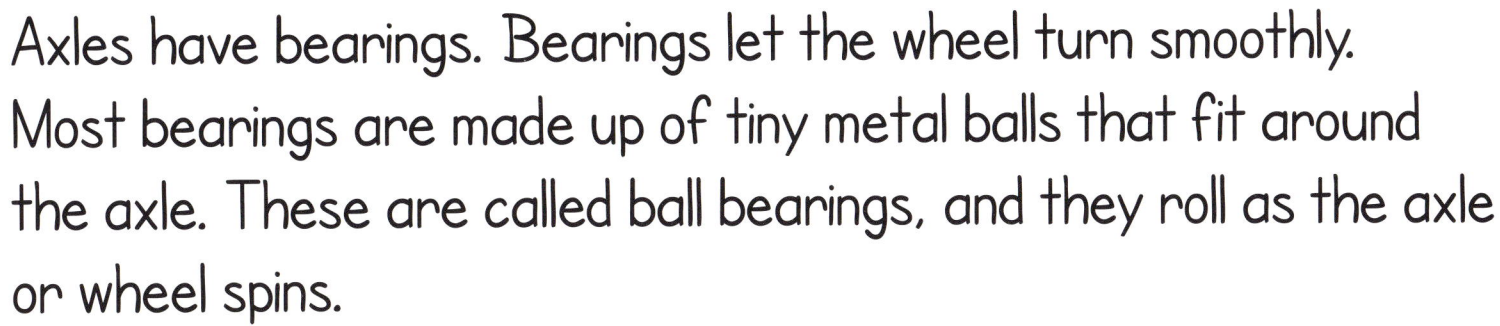

Axles have bearings. Bearings let the wheel turn smoothly. Most bearings are made up of tiny metal balls that fit around the axle. These are called ball bearings, and they roll as the axle or wheel spins.

Ball bearings

HOW A WHEEL WORKS

There is a part that makes the axle and wheel turn. This is different for every machine. In a bike, your feet and the pedals turn the wheels. In a car, the engine turns the wheels.

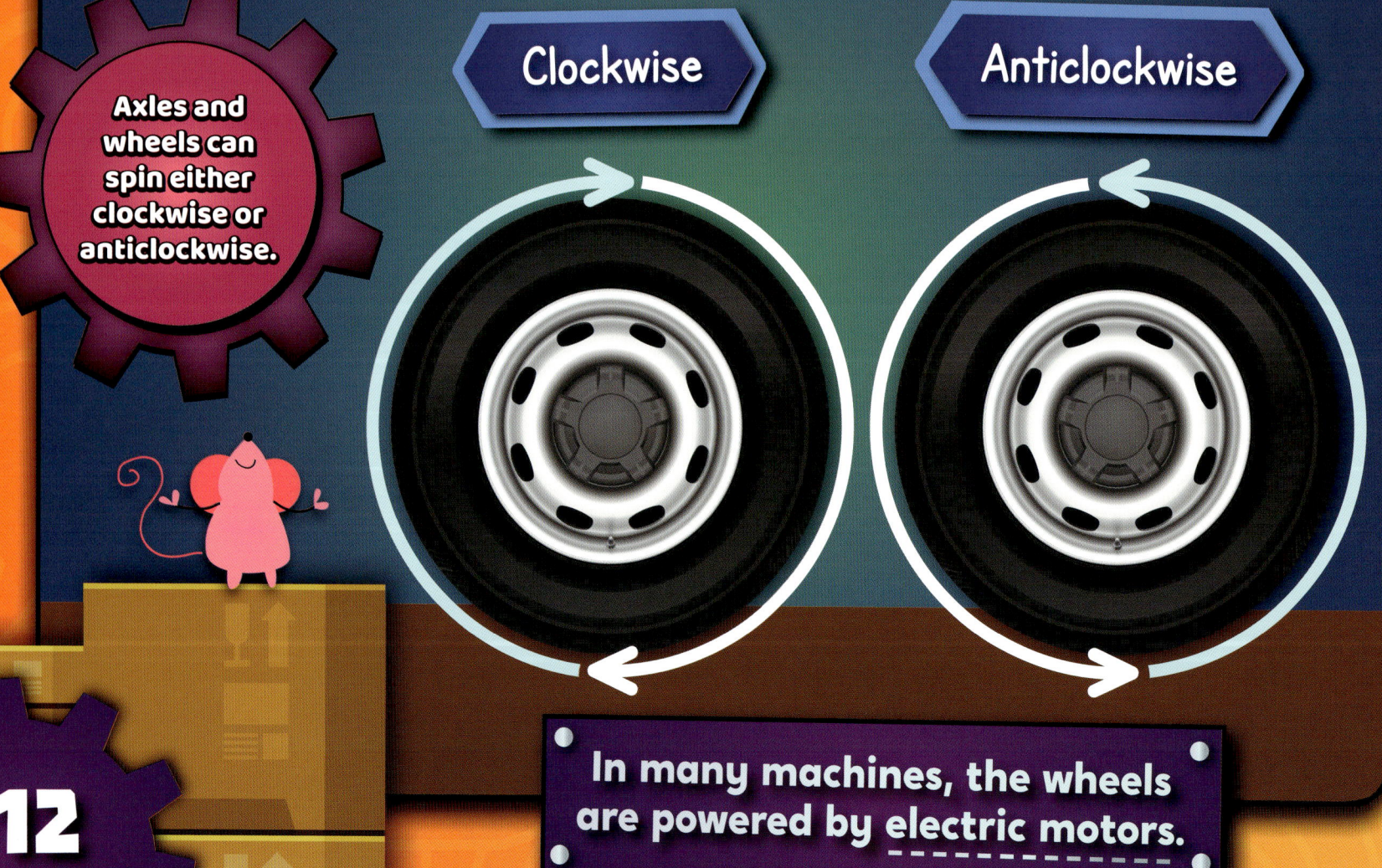

Axles and wheels can spin either clockwise or anticlockwise.

Clockwise

Anticlockwise

In many machines, the wheels are powered by electric motors.

Babhhejjjup!

Look how far people travel around the Ferris wheel and look how little the axle turns.

It is much easier to turn the axle instead of the whole wheel. This is why the wheel is useful. It can make things move farther with a smaller amount of <u>energy</u>.

FRICTION

Friction is a force caused by two things rubbing against each other. Friction stops things moving, and you need lots of energy to overcome it.

Every part of the bag touching the floor is causing friction. All the friction adds up.

Friction causes heat. It also causes things to be worn away over time.

Wheels help move things because they take away a lot of the friction. Only the bottoms of the wheels are touching the ground. The only other things touching are the axle and the wheel.

Less friction means things take less energy to move.

BETTER WHEELS

There are lots of ways to make wheels do even more work for even less energy. Usually this means getting rid of any friction.

Putting grease or oil on the axle helps the wheel to spin even more smoothly. Grease and oil make things slippery.

A road with an even surface allows the wheel to turn more easily. This makes it easier to drive on.

When a machine has big wheels, it means that the wheels work harder when the axle turns. However, wheels that are too big can cause all sorts of problems.

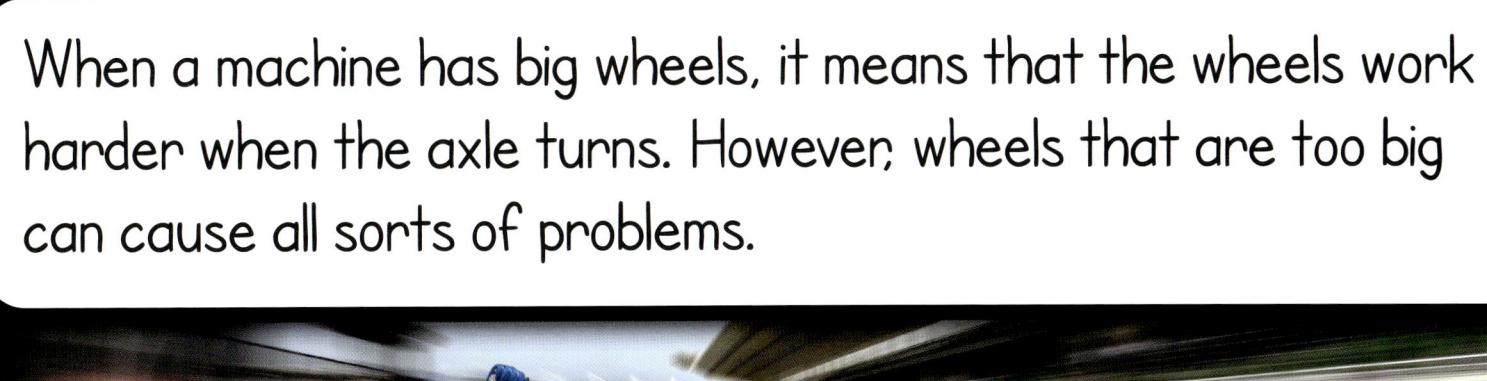

If the wheels on this racing car were too big, they would be heavy and hard to drive.

HUUUDVEEJUPFFF!

LET'S BUILD A TOY CAR

It is time to build! We will be using wheels to make a car that moves forwards on its own. You might want to get an adult to help you with the cutting, sticking and tying.

Heueghfluuph.

The car will move forwards using elastic bands.

YOU WILL NEED:

- 2 straws
- Glue
- 2 straight, thin wooden sticks, 30 centimetres long
- 2 straight, thin wooden sticks, 5 centimetres long
- 3 toothpicks
- Scissors
- 4 wheels (you can use bottlecaps with small holes in the middle)
- 3 elastic bands which are cut so they are straight lines
- 1 uncut elastic band

STEP 1

Place one smaller stick between the longer sticks so they make a three-sided rectangle and glue it down. This is the front. Glue the other smaller stick near the opposite end. This is the back.

STEP 2

Cut the straws so they are as long as the distance between the long sticks.

STEP 3

Glue a straw to each end of the long sticks. Make sure the straw is glued to both of the long sticks. Once dry, cut out the middle of the back straw.

STEP 4

Slide a toothpick through each straw. These are your axles. Stick a wheel on each end of the toothpicks.

STEP 5

Cut out a very small part of the final toothpick and glue it so it sticks out of the back axle.

STEP 6

Tie your three cut elastic bands into a line. Now tie one end to the front.

STEP 7

Tie the uncut elastic band to the end of the line and then loop it around the tiny bit of toothpick on the back axle.

STEP 8

It's ready! Now wind up the elastic bands by turning the back axle. Let go and watch it drive!

Make sure you have a smooth surface to drive on.

GLOSSARY

electric motors   machines that move things using electricity

energy   a type of power that can be used

force   a push or pull on an object

overcome   to defeat, overpower or deal with something

surface   the outside layer of something

universe   the space that everything exists in, including planets, galaxies and stars

vehicles   machines that have an engine and are used to carry people or things

INDEX

axles 7, 9–13, 15–17, 21–23
bearings 11
bikes 12
cars 5, 12, 17–18
doors 9
electricity 12
Ferris wheels 8, 13
friction 14–16
ground 6, 8, 15
machines 4–5, 9, 12, 17
roundabouts 8
spinning 7, 11–12, 16